TEN

LAMA LHAKPA YESHE

TALES

CULTIVATING

FROM

COMPASSION

TIBET

Wise poets that wrapped truth in tales
Knew her themselves through all her veils

from *'Know, Celia, Since Thou Art So Proud'*
by THOMAS CAREW

First published in the UK and North America in 2017 by

Leaping Hare Press

An imprint of The Quarto Group
The Old Brewery, 6 Blundell Street
London N7 9BH, United Kingdom
T (0)20 7700 6700 F (0)20 7700 8066
www.QuartoKnows.com

Text © 2017 Lama Lhakpa Yeshe
Photographs © 2017 Matthieu Ricard
Design and layout © 2017 Quarto Publishing plc

British Library Cataloguing-in-Publication Data
A catalogue record for this book is available from the British Library

ISBN: 978-1-78240-528-3

This book was conceived, designed and produced by

Leaping Hare Press

58 West Street, Brighton BN1 2RA, United,Kingdom

Publisher Susan Kelly
Creative Director Michael Whitehead
Commissioning Editor Monica Perdoni
Development Editor Viv Croot
Design JC Lanaway

Printed in Slovenia

10 9 8 7 6 5 4 3 2

The photographs in this book are by Matthieu Ricard, a Buddhist monk,
author, translator and photographer. They are used for illustrative purposes
only and are unconnected to the people, places and events in the stories.
Matthieu founded the humanitarian association Karuna-Shechen in 2000,
which provides health care, education and social services for the underserved
people of India, Nepal and Tibet. Please visit: http://karuna-shechen.org/

TEN

LAMA LHAKPA YESHE

TALES

CULTIVATING

FROM

COMPASSION

TIBET

FOREWORD BY SATISH KUMAR | PHOTOGRAPHY BY MATTHIEU RICARD

Leaping Hare Press

Contents

Foreword

Lama Lhakpa Yeshe is a teacher of compassion. Of course, all Buddhist teachers are teachers of compassion but for me Lama Lhakpa is special. He is humble and has a great sense of humour. He is the embodiment of compassion.

Suffering is just as fundamental and natural to every human being as joy is. However, when someone is joyful it is easy to join in the celebration of their happiness, but when someone is depressed and despondent, physically ill or mentally traumatized, people often look the other way. People don't want to know about other people's problems, as they are too busy with their own affairs. So making oneself available to others at a time of need is the most altruistic and selfless act one can perform. If that act is performed merely out of duty, or because it is a profession, then it is only a job. But when one is moved by compassion and is able to leave behind one's own affairs and devote oneself to the well-being of others, then that is a great example of freedom from a self-centred mind.

From the Buddha to Jesus Christ, from Lao Tzu to Mohammed and from Mother Teresa to Mahatma Gandhi, all great teachers have shown the way of compassion.

Ideals such as love, non-violence, mercy, peace, service, generosity and other similar great values help us to live a life of harmony and happiness. But these are the softer and somewhat easier paths. The path of compassion is much harder because we are required to share in the suffering of others. Although it is a much harder path to tread, it has been described as a royal road that can bring an end to ego and isolation.

When we place ourselves in the service of others, we realize the commonality of our lives. As the Buddhist teachings proclaim:

The sun is shining on everyone
no discrimination, no discrimination
The rain it falls on everyone
no discrimination, no discrimination
The earth has place for everyone
no discrimination, no discrimination
My heart has space for everyone
no discrimination, no discrimination
This is a song of compassion.

When we truly practise compassion, we realize that there need be no distinction between one living being and another. We are all related, we are all connected, we are all made from the same elements. When our heart is full of compassion, we feel the pain of the other in the same way as when our toe is hurt and our hand leaps to soothe the pain – the hand does not consider why it needs to soothe the pain in the toe. The hand and the toe are members of one body. Similarly, all human beings are members of one community. When we have that realization in the depth of our consciousness, then we are able to help others without hesitation. Out of such compassion emerges all other ideals, such as love, peace, harmony and generosity.

A society ruled by compassion will be free of human exploitation, racialism, sexism and all kinds of social discrimination. Compassion is the foundation and fundamental to a spiritual way of life.

Compassion is the road to enlightenment. Compassion is the source of justice, freedom, equality and peace.

In order to practise compassion for others, we need to have compassion for ourselves. Being kind to oneself is not selfish. Some individuals are very critical of themselves. Although self-criticism has a place, it should be built on self-compassion, self-care and self-nourishment.

Compassion for oneself and for other people should extend to compassion for all sentient beings. We need to show our compassion to animals, forests, oceans, to the entire planet Earth and the entire biosphere. Polluting oceans with plastics, cutting down rainforests and depriving the indigenous people of their livelihood, poisoning the soil with chemicals and pesticides, and emitting greenhouse gases that cause climate change are all acts of violence.

The Buddhist ideal of compassion extends to all living beings, human beings as well as other than human beings. Sometimes this ecological compassion is overlooked. In order to practise threefold compassion, we need compassion for ourselves, compassion for other people and compassion for the natural world. This is a seamless compassion continuum.

These ten tales, narrated by Lama Lhakpa Yeshe, are all about compassion. In Tibet, these stories are told and retold over generations. They are part of the oral tradition of storytelling, which serves to communicate the ideals of harmony and peace

Lama Lhakpa Yeshe comes to stay with us two or three times a year and he has been telling us these stories during his visits. Although these are traditional Tibetan tales, Lama offers them with his own particular angle. My wife, June, and I have been touched by their profoundness and simplicity. We are delighted that they are now made available to a wider audience.

Lama Lhakpa Yeshe was born in Tibet. He lived in a cave in Rewalsar, near Dharamsala in the Himalayas, for eight years, practising meditation, as well as studying Buddhist philosophy with various teachers including the Dalai Lama. During this period of prolonged solitude, he was invited to England and he began teaching in London, Lincoln, York and Liverpool. Now he travels between Europe, India and Nepal.

It has been a privilege to know this gracious lama and to learn from him the wisdom of compassion through these stories. It is my hope that these tales will inspire you, the reader, to put this great virtue into practice.

SATISH KUMAR

Introduction

My first encounter with Lama Lhakpa Yeshe was in 2004 while I was attending a mindfulness meditation course in London. There, sitting at the back, was a Tibetan monk politely watching the teacher explain how to count the breath. My first thought was: why does a Tibetan monk need to learn how to count the breath – and why here in Hackney?

After the class, I went over to find out. At this point, I might add that over all the years I have known Lama Lhakpa Yeshe, very few of his answers have ever been straightforward. And that's not to say Lama Lhakpa Yeshe's answers aren't clear, they certainly are; but rather, on a deeper level, the ideological differences between cultures can result in an abundance of further questions as opposed to answers. Or, to put it another way, his answer was that he was a refugee from Tibet and after some years of meditating in a cave in India he came to the UK.

This certainly didn't appease my overtly rational brain, but what it did do instead was begin a very rich and precious introduction into another way of looking at the world. And perhaps that's what's so valuable about the stories inside this intimate little book. They don't necessarily adhere to what we already know but instead offer us an opportunity to examine and explore new ways of being.

In those first encounters, I think Lama Lhakpa Yeshe and I were both students – I had no experience of Tibet's unique approach to Buddhism and he had little experience in teaching Western students. Analysis and critique seemed to be the hallmarks of my education, and patience and humour the legacy of his.

It was a blessing that I became acquainted with the motivation and discipline provided by a monastic style of learning, and looking back, I think we were lucky that neither of us took a closed attitude to each other's worlds. This is also perhaps a useful perspective to hold while visiting the places described in this book – these are not historically accurate depictions of locations, but this doesn't mean they lack substance. They are, instead, part of a long and rich oral tradition that uses storytelling as a tool for contemplation.

I have heard some of these stories many times and each time they vary – a mix of tale, orator and audience, a delicate balance that is needed to convey the subtle and complex concepts found in Tibetan Buddhism. Some of the tales can be seen as warnings. They don't venerate esoteric mantras or secret teachings but gently help us to pay more attention to our thoughts and emotions. This shift, a non-judgemental gaze inwards, is the means by which we can find the value of these tales.

One of the gifts of this book is the reminder, ultimately, that we have to take responsibility for our own lives. Both our successes and failures lie within our own actions. And it is in this light I believe Lama Lhakpa Yeshe offers these tales. It is through them that he invites us to deepen and enrich our relationship with ourselves and the world beyond.

SAM WINSTON
Author, artist and early student of Lama Lhakpa Yeshe

My Story *by Lama Lhakpa Yeshe*

I was born on 21 January 1967 in a town called Derge, at the heart of the historic Kham province of East Tibet. Derge is a centre of Buddhist culture, a town of monasteries. My uncle, Lama Guru Chowang, was a member of one of them. I liked him very much and respected him even more. From a very early age I wanted to be like him, I wanted to become a lama. I was only nine years old at that time, so my family was naturally concerned about my welfare, but I was very determined and persuaded them that it would be all right, as I would be joining the same monastery as my uncle, and would be under his care. My family finally agreed and I was allowed to join the 300 or so monks at Zigar Monastery.

An Early Lesson

The meditation practice at Zigar was very rigorous. Often we would have one or even two weeks of constant chanting and recitation for ten to twelve hours a day, with only short breaks for lunch and dinner. When I first joined the monastery, I did not question such strenuous practice, but by the time I was fourteen, I started to feel some kind of boredom and stress. I wanted to escape from such hard work.

On one occasion, I decided to pretend to be sick. This particular meditation course was ten days long. I had already participated for six days, and by the seventh day, I had had enough. I told my fellow students that I did not feel well and would not be attending the remaining sessions. For a whole day I lurked in my room, which was part of my uncle's quarters. There I discovered that even though I found the long periods of meditation boring, it was even more boring being on my own, in my room, away from the other monks.

I cast about for something to do. I had a very beautiful soft jacket made of fine lambswool. I'd been wearing it for quite a while and it was starting to look dirty so I decided to walk to a nearby stream with a hot spring to wash it. While I was washing my precious jacket, my classmates came outside for a short break from their meditation. Some of them, including a senior lama, spotted me scrubbing away. I saw them looking at me. Deeply embarrassed, I quickly gathered up my wet jacket and ran back to my room. I knew that they would come to find me and tell me off for ducking out of the meditation sessions, so I hastily arranged some bottles of medicine by my bed, pulled the blanket up over myself and lay with my eyes shut tight, pretending to be asleep.

Two or three lamas came to my room. They were very angry. 'You can't be sick, we saw you by the stream! Come along, you are not allowed to miss meditation.'

'Look, here are my medicines,' I croaked, feebly flapping my fingers at the row of bottles by my bed. 'I am feeling very poorly. Please go away and let me rest.'

They went away but they complained to my uncle. How could Lhakpa Yeshe be sick, they asked, if he is able to go to the stream and wash his jacket? They told my uncle to take me to the meditation hall; I should not miss such an important session. My uncle was very upset, even angry. With a stick in his hand, he burst into my room and scolded me, 'How can you allow yourself to be absent from such a significant ceremony when all the lamas are diligently participating in it?' I had nothing to say in my defence, so I followed him sheepishly to the meditation hall and rejoined all the others.

I tell this story only to highlight the fact that the practice of meditation is not always straightforward. It requires patience, diligence and commitment over a long period. Throughout my time at Zigar, I went through various ups and downs, doubts and difficulties, but I managed to stay steady on the path and eventually the state of meditation became second nature. After 25 years of practice, I felt at ease and comfortable with my life as a lama.

Journey to India

When I was 34, I was told that a senior lama from our order in India was looking for a number of monks to help and support him in the running of his monastery. I and six others from Zigar were asked to pack our bags and get ready to go. The idea of going to India and helping our monastery there was attractive and wonderful but the execution of it was full of problems and hazards.

The Chinese administration in Tibet would not allow anyone to travel to India officially. We had to go on foot, secretly and illegally, without passports. We were seven monks ready to go on this dangerous journey. Four laywomen and three laymen agreed to join us, one of whom knew the terrain and offered to act as our guide. We packed our rucksacks with food and clothes and got ready to go. My rucksack weighed 35 kilos!

In summer, even on the remote route we had chosen, there would be Chinese officials and Tibetan herders who would spot us travelling, so the only way we could escape without being noticed was to make the journey in winter. We passed through the populated areas and then travelled across the wild high plateau. It took us ten days to reach the border, and to escape the attention of Chinese officials and border guards, we walked at night and slept during the day. We walked through cold winds and snowstorms. We would sleep on the snow, huddled together, keeping each other warm as much as we could. (After we had entered Nepal and we could go to sleep at dusk, we would wake up to find the night's snowfall had covered us. At dawn, we would sit and chant, 'May we be safe, may all beings be safe, may we reach our destination alive . . .')

After many days travelling in Tibet, a local shepherd, sympathetic to our cause, told us that we should keep walking directly ahead, on and on, until we reached a high mountain, then we were to turn right and go around the mountain, where we would find a pass.

We followed these instructions and at last reached the pass, which was slippery with ice. Every time we tried to climb the pass, we would slip back, then we would try again. We were all terrified. For four or five hours, we made slow and arduous efforts. Finally, we arrived at the top of the pass and from there we saw spread out below us the land of Nepal, free of snow. We ran downhill with delight and excitement.

We were welcomed by the Nepalese and also met a number of Tibetan refugees living in Nepal. They helped us with fresh provisions. The journey from our monastery in Tibet to Kathmandu had taken 26 days. After a short rest, we set off again, and finally, after another month, we made it to India, to Rewalsar in the Himachal Pradesh and our monastery there.

In addition to supporting and helping our monastery, I began to practise meditation in total solitude in the cave that I lived in. The practice that had seemed so arduous in my youth in Zigar had now become compelling. Altogether I spent eight years in India, of which six were mostly spent meditating in the same cave. From time to time I attended teachings by His Holiness the Dalai Lama.

Coming to Europe

During this time, Nebojsa and Josipa, a devout Buddhist couple from Croatia, were among those who visited me. We established a close rapport and an intimate connection. They were my first European friends and students. One day, Nebojsa said to me, 'There are people in Croatia we know who would greatly benefit from learning Buddhist meditation and the way of compassion. Are you prepared to travel to Croatia and help them in their seeking?'

I thought long and hard about this. After a number of conversations, my Croatian friends persuaded me and arranged my travel to their country. Thus, I came to Europe. One thing led to another. More and more people wanted me to help them with the practice of meditation, and I gradually extended my travels in Europe, eventually taking up residence in England.

The Chinese invasion has brought colossal hardship to people in Tibet but the silver lining of this catastrophe is that it has at the same time brought great benefits to those outside Tibet. I am delighted to be a part of this movement.

I have discovered that there is in the West a profound and widespread interest in learning the philosophy and practice of Tibetan Buddhism. The essence of Buddhist teaching is to cultivate compassion to address all our problems, be they personal, political, social or environmental. Compassion is key to opening everyone's hearts and minds. Only through compassion can we find joy, peace and happiness.

LAMA LHAKPA YESHE

Black and White Pebbles

Once there was a young disciple whose mind was full of negative thoughts about his parents. He saw them as bossy and controlling, and he was always arguing with them; yet he was afraid of confronting them. The negative thoughts rolled around his mind like pebbles in a bowl, until he didn't know which way to turn. In turmoil and despair, he went to see the lama.

'My mind is full of anger and fear, dear Lama. What should I do about it?'

'Ah,' said the lama, 'the first step is to be aware of the state of your mind. Then you can overcome your anger, your fear and all your negative emotions.'

'How can I become aware of the state of my mind?' asked the disciple.

'Try this simple technique,' suggested the lama. 'Go to a mountain stream and collect twenty small pebbles. Take them home and spread them out on a table in front of you, then get a black bowl and

a white bowl. Put the white bowl on your left and the black bowl on your right. Sit still, close your eyes and observe the movement of your mind. Whenever a negative thought arises, open your eyes and put a pebble in the black bowl. Whenever a positive thought arises, open your eyes and put a pebble in the white bowl. Practise this for one week, then come and tell me how you get on.'

This seemed a simple, practical solution to the disciple's troubles and he was very pleased to learn about it. He thanked the lama and rushed home, collecting twenty small pebbles on the way. Once back home, he found a black bowl and a white bowl, went to his room, sat down and began following the lama's instructions.

As soon as he started observing his mind, he remembered his last argument with his parents and started fuming to himself that they were altogether too bossy and interfering. As a result, he felt angry with his parents, but also frightened of facing them. Then he realized that he was holding negative emotions towards his parents. One pebble in the black bowl. He wriggled on his seat and settled himself again, but his mind was still irritated. Another pebble in the black bowl.

Then he felt that he ought to give his parents a piece of his mind. Show them that they were not in charge of him. Another agitated thought – one more pebble in the black bowl. Half an hour passed quickly and at the end of it, the disciple discovered that all twenty pebbles were in the black bowl. This made him even more angry – but there were no pebbles left to record this. He stomped off to bed, his mind still full of anger and fear.

Next day he remembered that the lama had told him to use this technique for a whole week, so he tried again. His negative emotions were still too strong to control. He said to himself, 'Perhaps I should leave home, then my parents will realise how useful I am.' One pebble in the black bowl. Then he mused, 'No, I can't leave home, my parents are too old and frail to look after themselves.' A kind thought. The first pebble for the white bowl. 'But it's too difficult for me to manage my parents and live with them.' A negative thought. A pebble in the black bowl. 'But when I was small, I was naughty and yet my parents still looked after me and loved me.' A positive thought. A pebble in the white bowl. 'I am going to express my gratitude to them,' he resolved, 'and try to be patient with them.' Two pebbles in the white bowl. Half an hour passed. This time, at least, there were some pebbles in the white bowl. The disciple felt a certain sense of relief.

The third, fourth, fifth and sixth days passed. This exercise was proving very helpful; not only was the disciple watching his mind, he was also discovering a spirit of generosity within his heart. His conversations with his parents were becoming gentler.

When he woke up on the seventh day, he went eagerly to his bowls and pebbles. The very first moment of meditation brought a joyful thought. 'Thanks to my parents that I exist!' Pebble in the white bowl. 'How grateful I am to be in such good health.' Pebble in the white bowl. 'So good to have a roof over my head, and delicious food prepared by my mother on my plate.' More pebbles in the white bowl. Thought after thought was steeped in the positive emotions of humility, generosity, acceptance and love. Pebble after pebble after pebble dropped into the white bowl.

At the end of this meditation, the black bowl was empty and the white bowl was full.

Next day, the disciple went to thank the lama. The lama said to him, 'It is not the world that is the problem, it is our negative response to the world – so the way to be happy is to allow compassion to emerge

in the heart. Once compassion has arisen, we need to take care of it and maintain it. And then we must work diligently to make compassion flourish and grow larger and larger, so that every hour of the day, every day of the week, every week of the month and every month of the year is full of compassion and there is no room whatsoever for jealousy, anger, greed or fear.'

2   Shoes for the Mind

There was once a village in Tibet where everyone walked barefoot. The terrain around the village was rough and rocky, rugged and thorny, icy and cold. The villagers' feet were covered in cuts, bruises and sores, and bristled with spiky splinters.

Eventually, tired of suffering, they gathered together to discuss the problem. 'We have yaks,' someone pointed out, 'and when they die we have their skin. Why don't we lay that skin on the rugged paths? Then we'll be able to walk more easily.' This seemed to be an idea with merit, so they collected all their hides together and began to pave the way with leather; but they soon discovered, of course, that all the leather in Tibet would not be enough to cover the paths they had to tread. They wondered what to do.

'Let's go to the Great Master who lives in the monastery at the top of the mountain,' suggested a few people, 'and ask him what we should do.' Everyone thought this an excellent idea, so the whole village climbed the mountain to the monastery. It was a long way up, and some of them were quite breathless by the time they got there; but there was still breath enough to pose their question to the Great Master.

'Dear Lama, we have a big problem. We don't know whether you can help. Our problem is with our paths. We wanted to cover them with leather but we don't have enough. What should we do?'

'Ah,' said the Great Master. 'That is not a big problem. Let me think and I will give you the answer. Everybody, please sit down and we can meditate for five minutes. Just be present.'

After five minutes, the Master said, 'Everybody, open your eyes.' Then he smiled and gave his answer. 'It is not the paths that are the problem. It is us. Perhaps you should cover your feet with yak leather rather than trying to cover the paths of the land? You'll find that when you put leather on your feet they will be protected wherever you go. But don't forget that ending the suffering caused by bleeding feet is not enough. Like the rough and thorny roads, there are rough and thorny people in the world. They cause a lot of mental problems for us. When we meet those we find annoying and irritating, we must learn to cover our minds with compassion and patience, then we are freed from the problem.

'You have to end your mental suffering. Remember that just as you put on leather shoes to protect your feet, you need to put on shoes of compassion and patience to protect your mind. Then you will be calm and peaceful, and you will have tranquillity and harmony in your lives. Wherever you go your life will be easy, physically as well as mentally. You can't control the world, but you can control your negative response to it.'

The villagers were both touched and impressed by this advice. They went back down the mountain and set about making themselves yak leather shoes, which they wore every day; and whenever they felt irritated or annoyed, they reminded each other: 'Where are your shoes of patience and compassion?'

3   Inner Temple, Outer Temple

There was once a lama called Geshe Ben, who lived in a very modest hermitage in a small village in Tibet. He looked after a small temple and the people living nearby; they led a simple life and worked hard, and the temple was plain and unpretentious and just a little bit shabby.

A wealthy merchant living in a nearby town heard people praise Geshe Ben for his profound knowledge and wisdom, so he sent a messenger to the lama, asking if he could visit him and benefit from his teachings. Geshe Ben was surprised and pleased, and even rather flattered that such a visitor should come to his remote temple and hermitage. He thought that maybe the merchant might become a benefactor for the village . . . He sent the merchant a welcoming message and suggested that he came at the time of the next full moon – a very auspicious moment for the visit of such an esteemed guest.

Geshe Ben and the villagers began to prepare the temple for the merchant's arrival. There was much to do and they were very industrious, polishing the images of the Buddha, painting the walls, repairing the broken steps and giving the simple shrine a facelift.

But the night before the merchant was due to arrive, Geshe Ben tossed and turned in his bed, unable to sleep. He was sweating and very uncomfortable. What could be the matter? Was he ill? Then he realized that for the past few days he had paid very little attention to his Inner Temple. He had not given his usual amount of time to meditation, chanting and study, because his every waking hour had been devoted to decorating the village temple to impress the visiting merchant. What kind of intention was that? It was certainly not a pure intention.

The realization shocked him. He had been paying attention to the Outer Temple at the expense of the Inner Temple – and what is the good of having a shrine that shines on the outside when the purity of the shrine within is ignored?

In the morning, Geshe Ben got up and gazed at the beautiful glittering temple, the burnished Buddha and the pristine painted walls. Then he snatched up a basket full of dust and ash and scattered it energetically all over the Buddha's altar, making the temple look shabby and dowdy once again.

Soon the merchant and the villagers arrived and instead of welcoming them to the shrine, Geshe Ben led them to his hermitage, where they all sat in meditation, focusing on compassion and patience. After the silent meditation, Geshe Ben said, 'May we seek the precious mind of wisdom and compassion. Where such a mind is unborn, may it be born and when it is born may it be maintained and may it never decrease. May we always encourage wisdom and compassion to rise higher and higher so that all living beings may be liberated from suffering and may all beings be happy.'

The merchant was deeply inspired by the profound teaching and serenity of Geshe Ben. He resolved to practise compassion and seek wisdom, now and always. Moved by the experience, he made a generous gift of rice and barley to the village to celebrate the lama's teachings and the full moon.

Of course, as soon as the merchant left, the villagers, angry and puzzled, crowded around their lama. 'Geshe Ben, why didn't you show the visitor our lovely temple?' they demanded. 'And who's made it all dusty and dirty? Only yesterday we worked so hard cleaning it and now it's in a mess.'

Geshe Ben replied, 'Dear people, the true temple is within your heart. We must preserve our pure intentions. It is the purity of the mind and the heart that can bring an end to suffering. We should not be too concerned with the external temple. It is the internal temple that we should take care of.'

With that, the people of the village were satisfied, and their hearts were touched.

4   Medicine for the Mind

Not long ago, in a monastery in Tibet, there lived a learned lama who was full of wisdom. Many people came to listen to his spiritual teachings; he spoke about generosity of heart, compassion and loving kindness.

However, there was one young follower who was dissatisfied. He came to the lama and complained, 'Lama, I have been coming to you for more than a year now. I like the sound of your voice. I feel good in your company. Yet I have a problem. What you have to say about compassion and kindness is all very well but my life is still full of tension, stress, anger, fear and anxiety. Your teachings don't seem to have helped in any way.'

The lama replied, 'My dear friend, it is true that you have been listening to me for some time but it seems that my words have entered one of your ears and come out unheeded through the other. You have not even carried my teachings as far as your home and it certainly seems that you have not applied them to your life.'

'Dear Lama,' said the young man, 'I have to deal with my troublesome colleagues when I'm working, and when I get home I have to face my unruly children, my difficult wife, my uncooperative parents and my unfriendly neighbours. All your talk of kindness and compassion is just too idealistic and impractical for me.'

The lama replied, 'You are like a sick person who goes to a doctor. The sick person is happy to get diagnosed, to take the prescription to the chemist, to collect the medicine, to carry it home, but then complains that the medicine tastes too bitter or is too difficult to swallow or that they are too busy to remember to take it regularly. If a sick person is really serious about getting better and finding a cure for their disease, they have to make every effort to take their medicine regularly and follow the doctor's instructions about diet and exercise and the right amount of sleep. They have to change their habits and transform their lifestyle. Curing cancer or a heart problem or any other illness is a serious matter.

'In the same way, you must take my teachings to your heart and diligently apply the mental medicine of compassion, patience and generosity. I am a doctor of the mind. I prescribe meditation as a medicine for the mind. Just as medicine heals the body, meditation heals the mind and dispels the diseases of depression, tension, stress and anger. But, dear friend, you have to take the medicine. I can't take it for you. It's no good putting the prescription of compassion in your pocket and not using it. If your children, wife, parents, neighbours and colleagues are gentle and wonderful and you have no problems with your mind, then you don't need my mental medicine. But because you have emotional problems with other people, you have to heal yourself by sowing the seed of compassion in your heart. And when compassion is born, you must look after it as you would a little baby – nurture it, care for it and help it to grow and flourish. When your compassion is big and

strong, you will become resilient enough not to be disturbed by adverse circumstances.'

The young man could see that the lama was a good doctor of the mind, and acknowledged the truth in his explanation. He took the lama's teachings back to his home and into his heart, knowing it was up to him to take his 'medicine' and practise patience and compassion in his daily life.

5   Wind of Compassion

Once, a long time ago, there lived a great lama in Tibet, whose name was Patrul Rinpoche.

One day a man came to him and said, 'Great lama, I have been going from teacher to teacher, from temple to temple, and from book to book seeking peace and happiness. I have a fine house, I have land and I have money, but I am not happy. I have a good family, good neighbours and good friends, and still I have no peace of mind. What's wrong with me?'

And Patrul Rinpoche replied, 'You're looking in the wrong place. You are looking for peace and happiness outside yourself but they cannot be found outside. They are within you. Inside you there is pure mind, pure consciousness and pure spirit – like a beautiful mountain with a wonderful waterfall, fragrant flowers, graceful trees, sweet singing birds and colourful butterflies.

'However, this beautiful mountain of pure mind is concealed by clouds of fear, anger, anxiety, attachment and desires. These clouds prevent you from seeing your own pure mind, which is the true source of peace and happiness.'

'Then what can I do to discover the pure mind within me?' asked the man, in some distress. 'How can I see through the clouds?'

The lama replied, 'You need to create a great wind of compassion to blow away the clouds of ignorance, ego and self-centredness. You need to cultivate deep compassion for all sentient beings. The pure mind within will be revealed when you develop mindfulness and loving kindness through meditation. Then your own wisdom,

which is always within you, will generate the wind of compassion and eventually, little by little, the mountain of pure mind will be revealed and you will be able to enjoy the waterfalls of happiness and flowers of peace.'

'Thank you, lama, for this insight,' said the man, humbly, 'but this sounds very difficult. Could you please tell me some practical ways to develop compassion?'

'Well,' replied the lama, 'there are seven practical steps you can take in order to generate the wind of compassion.

'FOR THE FIRST STEP, think that you have been in this world for a long time and have gone through many births. During these cycles of life, at one time or another all creatures have been your mother, your father, your sister or your brother. Thus, you are related to all living beings, so treat every living being with respect and love as if they are your relatives. No one is an alien, no one is a stranger, everyone is kith and kin to you.

Thinking like this, you can be compassionate to all living beings.

'FOR THE SECOND STEP, remember that you have been helped and supported by others in this life and in previous lives. You have been given food, clothes, shelter and much more for your sustenance and nourishment. Without the kindness and generosity of others, you would not have survived.

Remembering like this, you can be compassionate to all living beings.

'FOR THE THIRD STEP, act. Now you are in a position to repay the kindness of others by being kind to them in return. You are in debt to other living beings. Now is your opportunity to serve others, to take care of others, to be generous to others, to be kind. Feel no arrogance or pride in giving. You are only repaying the debt.

Acting like this, you can be loving and compassionate to all living beings.

'FOR THE FOURTH STEP, learn the way to care for others from others. Look at how parent birds behave. They prepare a soft and secure nest to protect their eggs. When the egg is laid, the parent bird keeps it warm with its wings and its whole body. When the egg hatches and the chick is born, the parent bird hunts for food and feeds the chick from its beak. It gives all its attention, without distraction, to the care and well-being of the young. You can be like a parent bird for all living beings. The purpose of your life is to be kind to others. Only when you are kind to others will you be happy. *Behaving like this, you can be compassionate to all living beings.*

'FOR THE FIFTH STEP, engage with others. You may not always be capable of helping by yourself. When that happens, you can ask others to join you in helping living beings to be released from their suffering. Think of a mother – suppose she was unable to swim, and her child is being swept away by a river and is in danger of drowning. Of course, she cries out for help, for able-bodied strangers to leap into the river to save the child. Similarly, if you find any living being drowning in the sea of suffering through ignorance and attachment, you can seek help to liberate living beings from their suffering.

Engaging like this, you can be compassionate to all living beings.

'FOR THE SIXTH STEP, learn to be always impartial and calm and composed. Compassion cannot be selective. You need to let go of the idea that someone is your friend and someone is your enemy. Your kindness is offered equally, without any favour or discrimination, to one and all, regardless of gender, race, colour, religion or nationality. Everyone is a member of your family.

Impartiality like this can help you be compassionate to all living beings.

'FOR THE SEVENTH STEP, cultivate sympathetic joy in the success, happiness and achievements of others. Learn to be free of jealousy, resentment and irritation when you see someone else is blessed with recognition and accomplishments. Learn to celebrate the good fortune of others.

Sympathetic joy will help you be compassionate to all living beings.'

When he heard these seven simple steps of practical advice and guidance, the man who had been troubled was able to see the way forward to generate the wind of compassion in his heart. He thanked the lama, and got ready to leave; but the lama had one more piece of advice.

'These seven steps are like seven pills that I give you as spiritual medicine. Take them away with you, but remember that they will be no good if you put them away on a shelf and don't take them. They need to be taken every day. The daily practice of compassion is everything.'

The man was touched by this wisdom, and inspired by the seven steps to generating the wind of compassion.

6   Many Paths to Enlightenment

The great Tibetan lama Patrul Rinpoche was a widely revered and much respected teacher, and people gathered around him to receive his wisdom and insight. His teachings were simple, direct and profound, and in one way or another the essence of his discourse always led to the practise of compassion.

One day he said to a small group of his students: 'The purpose of life is to help all sentient beings to be free from suffering. In order to do this, you need to cultivate unconditional, unlimited and pure compassion towards all, without any exception.'

Patrul Rinpoche always encouraged discussion, debate and dialogue, so after making this all-embracing statement, he asked, 'Do you understand?'

One of the students had some questions. 'Are there not three ways to seek enlightenment? Should I first attain enlightenment for myself and then help others to enlightenment? Or should I work on my own enlightenment at the same time as helping others to enlightenment? Or should I assist others first and then work on my own enlightenment? Which is the better way? Please, Lama, would you explain it to us in a way we can't possibly misunderstand?'

Patrul Rinpoche smiled. 'Now, those are very good questions indeed,' he replied, 'and it depends on your own natural inclination. One way is similar to the way of a king or a queen or a great ruler. People in that position wish to acquire and accumulate power and wealth before helping and providing prosperity to everyone else. Like kings and queens, there are people who wish to become enlightened, to accomplish total purity of heart for themselves and

then go out in the world and help others to undertake the practice of compassion and kindness. They think to themselves, "Unless I am kind and compassionate myself, how can I help others achieve enlightenment?" So they work on themselves first and then they help others.

That, I call the way of the kings and queens.'

The lama paused and looked around at his students to make sure they had understood, then he continued: 'The second way is similar to the way of the captains of ships. Before they can start on their voyage, they must have everyone on board with them. Everyone makes the journey together and sails across the sea and arrives at the other shore together and at the same time. Like sea captains, there are people who act collectively. Their own enlightenment and practice of compassion go hand in hand with helping other people in their journey towards compassion.

That, I call the way of the sea captain.'

Patrul Rinpoche took a few deep breaths and surveyed his students again. They were all listening attentively. 'There is a third way,' he went on, 'the way of shepherds and cowherds. These people gather their animals and take them to green pastures in the summer. As you know, in winter time, because of the snow, sheep, cows and yaks are kept indoors, but in the summer farmers take their animals to the mountains. These herders of horses, mules, donkeys, yaks, cows, sheep and goats make sure that their animals are on lush fields, grazing happily. The fields are full of wild flowers, nourishing herbs and cool streams where the animals can drink. When the keepers see that their flocks are well settled and enjoying their grazing, safe from predators, then and only then do they relax, put up their yurts, cook their meals and rest in comfort. Similarly, there are seekers of enlightenment and compassion who help and assist other living beings to find fulfilment, contentment and wisdom. They care for others first, before seeking their own salvation. That, I call the way of the shepherds.'

Then Patrul Rinpoche left his students for a while to discuss the matter among themselves. They were soon in hot dispute.

'Surely the way of the kings and queens is best. How can we help others without being compassionate ourselves?' said one.

'No, no, no, I think the way of the sea captain is much better. We all have to work together. Then everyone is enlightened at the same time,' said another.

'I don't agree. In my view, the way of the shepherds is best. We have to help others before we help ourselves,' said a third.

When the lama returned, one student asked him, 'Rinpoche, please will you tell us which is the best way? We can't agree and we want to know for certain.'

'My dear students,' replied Rinpoche, 'there is no one way that suits everybody. As I said before, it depends on your character, your personality, your make-up. Whichever way you follow, as long as you follow a way, you will get there. Putting one way higher or better is a mark of discrimination and even arrogance. The way of the kings and queens, the way of the sea captain and the way of the shepherd are simply metaphors. They are like labels. There's no need to get stuck with labels. As long as you're cultivating compassion, you are on the right path. Thinking that one way is better than another, or that my way is better than your way, is a sign of ego. While seekers of truth pursue their own ways, they should always respect the ways of others.

'The way of wisdom and compassion makes you humble. Be like a stalk of barley with a head full of ripe grain, bending low with its weight. Bending low is a sign of fullness and maturity. A stalk without grain stands up, stiff and erect. It may appear strong and

upright but it has no grain, it gives little nourishment to anyone. Therefore, practise compassion with humility, be wise without arrogance. One can be arrogant in the name of religion, nationality, colour or gender. We need to free ourselves from these negative attitudes that divide us from each other and instead practise the way of compassion.

'So follow whichever way comes naturally to you. It is not the external form of practice that matters, it is the inner spirit, the pure mind, that we need to pay attention to.'

7   A Tale of Two Beggars

The revered lama Patrul Rinpoche preached to his followers every day and sometimes, to help make his teaching easier to understand, he told parables and stories. One day, he decided to tell his students the tale of two beggars, and they gathered round him to listen.

'Whether you are rich or poor, what really matters is the state of your heart and mind,' said Patrul Rinpoche. 'If your heart is pure and kind and your mind is noble and humble, then even external conditions can change in your favour.' He looked around at his students, paused for a few moments to make sure they were all listening, then began.

'There were once two beggars living in the city of Lhasa. Let's call them Cheerful Beggar and Miserable Beggar. One day, as they were begging in the town square, they heard the news that a very wealthy man was going to put on a great feast at his grand house for the lamas from the big monastery.

'The Miserable Beggar (who was very greedy and selfish) said, "Right. I'm going to go to this rich man's house before the lamas get there and I'll get the very best food before they have a chance to fill their bellies. Serves them right."

'The Cheerful Beggar replied, "Do what you like, but I'm going to wait until after the lamas have eaten and gone back to the monastery. I'm sure there'll be lots of food left and certainly I'll get some of it."

'"You stupid beggar," sneered the Miserable Beggar, "what's the point of turning up when the very best food is finished? Why should the lamas get all the good stuff?"

'So he left the Cheerful Beggar behind and scuttled off to the wealthy man's house. Armies of cooks and their assistants were delivering huge platters of delicious delicacies of all kinds – shimmering heaps of saffron rice, enormous bowls full of lentils and vegetables glistening with butter, mouthwatering confections of almonds and honey, vats of creamy yoghurt . . .

The Miserable Beggar sat down by the entrance gate, smacked his lips in anticipation and began pestering for food; but there were several guards at the gate, and a couple of them strolled menacingly over to the Miserable Beggar. "Move on, beggar. Don't you know that the revered lamas will be here soon for their meal? We don't want people like you littering the place."

'The Miserable Beggar – who was foolhardy as well as selfish and greedy – spat back at them, "You stupid fools, why are you stopping me? You have to give me food. I'm starving!"

"No way," said the guards. "No one eats before the lamas. Now get out of here before we throw you out." They were very big guards; and the Miserable Beggar, disappointed and dejected, had to go away with an empty begging bowl, an even emptier stomach and darkness in his heart. Scowling and shouting, and shaking his fist, he made his way back to the town square, where the Cheerful Beggar was still sitting peacefully.

"Don't waste your time going up there," snarled the Miserable Beggar, "they're never going to give you anything. They are all mean and selfish."

"'OK, OK, don't be so angry,' said the Cheerful Beggar. "We have to know our place. Beggars can't be choosers, as they say. I'll wait until the feast is over and the lamas have gone." The Miserable Beggar rolled his eyes and snorted.

'A few hours passed and at last, from far away, the Cheerful Beggar saw the lamas leaving the wealthy man's house. When they had all departed, he got up, leaving the Miserable Beggar fuming, made his way to the entrance gate of the house, and spoke very humbly to the guards. "Sirs, if there is any food left over, may this poor man be also fed? I will bless you from the bottom of my heart. I know the wealthy man is very kind and generous, he has fed all the lamas of the monastery so well, may he be blessed!"

'When they heard such gentle words from the beggar, the guards at the gate were very touched. "Of course, there's plenty of food left over. Wait here a minute and we'll bring you some." Soon a huge bowl full of delicious-smelling food was brought to the Cheerful Beggar, and he was very happy and grateful. He walked back with the brimming bowl to the Miserable Beggar and said, "Here it is, here you are, let me share my food with you."

'The Miserable Beggar was astonished. How could this be? "They were really mean and harsh to me, how come they were so generous to you?" he asked suspiciously.

"'Don't worry about it," shrugged the Cheerful Beggar. "I don't know the answer. Come and eat the food while it's still hot." They sat down together to eat, and as they were relaxing after their sumptuous meal, the Miserable Beggar asked the Cheerful Beggar,

"Suppose one day you became the ruler of the land, what changes would you make?"

'The Cheerful Beggar thought about it, and smiled. "I have no wish to become a ruler, but if by any chance that were to happen, I'd feed the hungry first so that no one in my country would need to be a beggar. Then I'd build enough houses for the poor so that no one would need to be homeless and cold. I'd provide enough places where the sick could be restored to good health and I'd build schools where children could learn ethical values, to be kind and gentle and have practical skills for right livelihood."

"'You dreamer!" scoffed the Miserable Beggar. "What's the point in all that? Now, if I had power and wealth, I'd build grand palaces for myself. I'd have buckets of gold and silver and diamonds in my treasury. I'd train specialist armed guards to protect me. I'd punish all those who disobeyed me and I'd conquer other lands to accumulate an even greater amount of wealth."

'The Cheerful Beggar smiled even more broadly and said, "Oh dear. Your dream and mine are so incompatible there's no point in us staying together, so I suggest we part company." So they said goodbye and went their separate ways.

'The Miserable Beggar obsessed to himself. He kept thinking, "Is there any way I can kill the king and become wealthy and powerful myself? I can't spend all my life begging, homeless and cold." But he could find no way of fulfilling his desire. Sometimes he got food from begging, sometimes he had to scrabble to find food on rubbish heaps. He lived a miserable life in anguish and discontent. The constant lack of food and the cold climate wore him down and he became ill. There was no one to care for him, he had no friends. Finally, he died, alone, disheartened and in pain.

'But the Cheerful Beggar travelled here and there, smiling and contented, finding sufficient food and clothes to keep his body and soul together. One day during his travels he came to a land where the local chief had just passed away. In that land, tradition dictated that oracles be consulted and ambassadors sent out to look for a new chief with miraculous powers. The Cheerful Beggar knew nothing of this. He was pleasantly tired after his long walk, so he settled down contentedly under a tree to rest and began to doze off. After a while, a search party of frantic ambassadors passed by. They were amazed to see that the tree was in full blossom while all the other trees around were bare due to a severe winter, and behind the tree there was a double rainbow, even though there had been no rain. They approached the tree and found a man whose face was full of grace, and who had the appearance of peace and a kind heart.

'Putting all the signs and omens together, they decided that this was the right man to become the chief of their people, so they asked the Cheerful Beggar, "Who are you? Do you possess some powers to make the tree blossom in winter and a rainbow appear without any hint of rain?"

'"No," smiled the Cheerful Beggar. "I am nothing but a humble and ordinary man. I've no idea why this tree is in blossom or why there's a double rainbow in the sky when there has been no rain."

'"We are very touched by your humility," said the ambassadors. "You are so gracious and peaceful. Our chief, who was a very benevolent ruler, has just passed away. We are searching for a new chief and we're certain we have found one in you."

'The Cheerful Beggar was very surprised and could not believe that this was reality. Maybe I'm dreaming, he thought to himself. The ambassadors were eager to persuade him and very insistent, so sure were they that he was the one: "Please accept our invitation and be our chief."

'Eventually the Cheerful Beggar smiled and said, "If I can be of any help or of service to you, I am at your disposal." So he became the chief of that land and fulfilled his wish to feed the poor, house the homeless, heal the sick and educate the children. Many, many years later he died, contented and fulfilled.

'This story shows that kindness of heart and purity of mind can and do make you happy within yourself and prosperous without,' concluded Rinpoche. 'Kindness and compassion are not only great spiritual ideals, they are a way to a happy life in this world, in the here and now.'

The students were delighted with the tale, and with Patrul Rinpoche's teaching, for which he became even more famous in his country.

8   Learning from Loss

The great lama Dipankara was a much loved and admired teacher with many students and followers. People in Tibet lived at that time in small settlements scattered around the country, so Dipankara would travel from place to place teaching about compassion, kindness and generosity. In gratitude, his followers gave him horses, yaks, ornaments of gold and silver, warm clothes, good-quality shoes, plenty of food and numerous pots and pans – so the lama travelled with his entourage in apparent luxury.

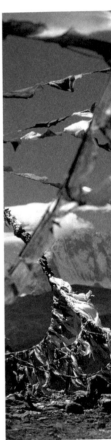

One day, some robbers saw the lama and his group on horseback, followed by yaks carrying the gifts and all the useful equipment. Bedazzled by all this wealth and all these objects of delight, the robbers plotted to steal them for themselves.

The next day, Dipankara was going on a long journey through mountains and valleys. It was lovely weather, and the group proceeded slowly to enjoy the beauty of it. Evening drew close before the lama could reach the settlement where his followers were waiting for him, so he and his party decided to camp in a beautiful clearing. They set up their tents, tethered their animals, made a camp fire, cooked some supper and went to bed happy and contented.

But high up on a ridge, the robbers were watching and waiting. Around midnight, when the lama and his companions were fast asleep, the thieves crept down, wrapped the sleeping travellers in their tents, bound their hands and feet tightly with ropes, and stole all their possessions and animals. They rode away, laughing, into the night. Nobody knew which way they went. Meanwhile,

Dipankara and his students, nearly suffocated by their tents and unable to move, had to wait helplessly for many hours for someone to free them from their suffering.

In the morning, the families in the settlement where the great lama was expected were perplexed, wondering why he and his party had not reached them. Eventually, a group of villagers set out in search of their lost teacher; they soon came across the camp and heard the faint, muffled shouts for help. Shocked and surprised, they quickly liberated the lama and his companions from their bondage and took them to their settlement, where they gave them a good meal and restored them to comfort and warmth.

Then a party of strong men set off to look for the gang who had treated their beloved teacher so harshly. Within a few days, the robbers were caught and arrested and taken into custody. All the horses, yaks and other equipment were recovered and brought back to the lama.

'Where did you find the robbers? And where are they now?' asked the lama eagerly.

'We found them hiding in a forest in one of our valleys. There was a struggle, but we managed to round them up, and now they are in police custody.' The villagers were rather proud of themselves.

'Please take me there. I want to meet the robbers,' said the lama. He was very insistent.

The people were puzzled. They could not understand why the lama was so keen to see the robbers who had inflicted so much pain on him. It seemed strange, and rather dangerous. However, he was their beloved teacher, and if that was what he desired, that is what they would do. The great lama was taken to meet the robbers, and the moment he caught sight of them, dejected and ashamed as they were, he asked for them to be freed, despite everybody's objections.

'These are not robbers or thieves, they are my teachers,' said the lama, calmly. 'Why did I have so many possessions? All they gave me was trouble and anxiety and caused attachment. These robbers and thieves are poor. They need our compassion and forgiveness. They also need this food and these clothes. They need land and shelter. We must be kind to them.'

Dipankara's command had to be obeyed, of course, as he was their revered teacher; but everybody understood the profound wisdom in what he was saying. So food and clothes were given back to the robbers and, under the supervision of the lama and the villagers, they were provided with land and livelihood. The robbers were surprised and amazed and at the same time delighted and grateful.

This story of extraordinary generosity, great compassion and a rare act of forgiveness spread far and wide. The robbers were not only liberated from their imprisonment, they were themselves transformed into great practitioners of compassion. This example demonstrated that evil and negativity can only be overcome by goodness and a positive act of love.

9 The Power of Belief

There once lived a woman in Tibet whose son was a trader who travelled extensively for his business. The woman was devoted to Buddha and his teachings, and also to her son. One day he said to her, 'Mother, I'm going to India to bring back merchandise of great value, so I'll be away for longer than usual. Please don't worry about me, and take care of yourself.'

His mother was overjoyed. 'India is a holy land,' she cried, 'it's the birthplace of our great teacher of compassion, the Buddha. Please will you do me a favour? In your travels, try to get to Bodh Gaya. There's a famous banyan tree there under which the Buddha sat for a long time meditating, and under that tree he was enlightened. Bring me a sacred relic from there. That will comfort me and delight me.'

'Of course, mother, I'll certainly do that,' said the son; it didn't sound too difficult a task.

And so he went to India, travelling here, there and everywhere for more than a month. He was so busy with his business that he forgot all about the relic his mother had asked him to get for her. In fact, he had no chance to visit Bodh Gaya at all, because he had no business interest there.

When he arrived home, his mother greeted him joyfully. She was very pleased to see him, and very excited about the kind of relic he could have brought. She waited for her son to say something. She waited in vain. After a while, she could wait no longer and so she asked, 'How was Bodh Gaya? Did you find a relic for me there?'

The son was filled with shame and embarrassment. Putting his palms together in humility, he confessed, 'Mother, I am very sorry but I was so preoccupied with my work that I completely forgot about what you asked for.' Then seeing how disappointed she was, he went on, 'But please don't worry, India is a great country full of wonderful merchandise, so I'll be going there again very soon. Next time, I'll remember what you asked and bring you a sacred relic.'

Of course, his mother was very understanding and forgiving. She loved her son very much; so she said to herself, 'I will wait with patience. I am sure he'll remember next time.'

Within a couple of months, all the goods the trader had brought from India were sold. Once again he came to his mother to ask her blessing for his journey to India. His mother said, 'Go well, travel safely and remember to visit Bodh Gaya. Promise me that this time you will bring me a relic from that sacred site.' And she smiled, to show she had faith in him.

'Yes, mother, I promise,' replied the son. And he really meant it . . .

He went to Varanasi, where he acquired delicate hand-woven silk. He went to Lucknow and acquired beautiful hand-crafted jewellery. He went to Kolkata and acquired brightly coloured cotton cloth. He came back with horses and mules loaded with all this and even more lovely things unavailable in Tibet. As he approached his village, very pleased to be getting home, he suddenly remembered his mother's heartfelt request for him to bring a sacred relic from Bodh Gaya – but he had brought nothing, because he had been completely immersed in his business. He could not think of facing

his mother without the relic she wanted so much. He was angry with himself. What could he do now? He sat down with all his horses, mules and men around him and thought. Nothing. So he went for a walk to see if that would bring him inspiration. He noticed the skeleton of a dead dog beside a cairn, and had a brainwave. He took a tooth from the dog's skull, wrapped it in a

khata (a traditional Tibetan offering scarf) of fine white silk and put it carefully in his breast pocket.

He arrived home, paid the men, led the horses and mules into his stable, stored his merchandise in the barn, and then came into the kitchen, where his mother was preparing a small feast for him.

She was very happy to see him, and hugged him to her. 'Welcome home, my son. You look thinner than before you went. Are you exhausted? Sit down and have some food.' As soon as he sat down he said, 'Mother, here is something very special for you, something very rare. I was very lucky to find it. I have brought you a tooth from the Buddha himself.'

His mother dropped the soup ladle. 'Oh, my son, how wonderful you are! Thank you! Thank you again and again,' she cried ecstatically, as she held the white khata with its sacred relic reverently in her hands. She was over the moon with joy, and filled with gratitude for her son. Placing the khata in the centre of her sacred altar, she lit a candle and some fragrant incense and began prostrating, reciting holy mantras. Now the Buddha, the great teacher of compassion himself, was in her house.

The son smiled with satisfaction. However he had done it, he had made his mother happy and it made him happy to see her so uplifted. The secret of his gift was known only to himself and no one else. He watched his mother day after day prostrating, meditating and chanting. She was kinder to him than ever before. She treated his friends, guests and customers with the utmost grace and hospitality. She gave food to the poor, consoled the grieving and offered compassion to everyone she met. The son witnessed something magical. He knew she felt great love and compassion for him, but now he saw her pour it out from her heart to encompass the whole world. He could not believe that a fake relic could have so much power to transform.

Because of the presence of this object, which for the mother was the living Buddha himself, she became free from all emotions of fear, pride and anger. An overwhelming devotion to the Buddha permeated every moment of her life. And as she was being transformed, something was happening on the altar itself, something unimaginable and magical.

One day, she decided it was time to look at the tooth of the Buddha with her own eyes. Until that moment she had practised restraint, but now she opened the khata and, lo and behold, she found two objects. One was the dog's tooth; the other was a human tooth, a tooth of the Buddha. No one knew where it came from but there it was. It was a miracle.

Tibetans recognize that the power of belief, of meditation, of prostration and positive intention is so great it can create miracles that cannot be explained by the rational mind. This inner power is comparable to the power of the sun. When the sun shines long enough, it can make ice melt and become a stream of sweet water. Therefore, spiritual teachings ask us to work hard and constantly on ourselves in order to reveal the power of positive belief.

The Wounded Dog

A long time ago, there lived in Tibet a boy called Tomi, whose mother was a devout follower of the Buddha. She practised meditation for her personal purification and compassion for the well-being of others.

One day the mother said to Tomi, 'My son, the best life is that in which one can realize nirvana, which is liberation from negative emotions such as anger, fear and pride. Giving birth, bringing you into this world was hard work. I hope you will not waste your life pursuing trivial matters, and that you will use this precious human life to accomplish self-realization.'

Tomi listened to his mother's words intently, both inspired and touched by the hope she had for him. Silently, within his heart, Tomi resolved that he would do everything he could to fulfil her dream for him.

That night, Tomi came to his mother and said, 'Mummy, you have given me a good idea. I am going to the mountains. I will live in solitude there and meditate until I meet Maitreya Buddha – the Buddha of compassion. When he appears to me, I will ask him to teach me the perfect way to become enlightened and serve all beings.'

His mother was delighted. She knew that Tomi was brave and strong-willed and that he would be able to overcome all hardships and difficulties that might come his way. She blessed him wholeheartedly and wished him well in his endeavour.

The next morning, Tomi set out and walked for many miles until he discovered a secluded cave in the mountains. Here he settled himself and started to meditate, visualizing Maitreya Buddha being present with him in the hope that his visualization would become real and that Maitreya Buddha would appear to him in person.

Shepherds, yak herders and nomadic people saw Tomi in meditation and, thinking that he was a holy man, they left small gifts of food. Month after month of meditation went by as Tomi waited eagerly for Maitreya to appear. Three years passed this way. Tomi lacked neither concentration nor dedication but he did not see Maitreya, and he became despondent. 'I'm wasting my time,' he thought. 'If after three years of patient waiting I have still not encountered Maitreya, there is no hope for me.' So he left the cave and started to walk back home.

On the way, he passed through a small settlement where he saw a man working very hard. The man had an enormous piece of metal that he was rubbing furiously. Tomi stood there flabbergasted, mesmerized by the man's industry. He kept rubbing the metal harder and harder. Tomi could resist no longer; he just had to ask. 'What on earth are you doing?'

'I need a needle,' replied the man, 'so I am working away at this metal until it becomes a needle.'

That answer made Tomi think deeply. He reflected that perhaps three years of meditation was not long enough. 'If this man has the patience to work long and hard to turn a huge piece of metal into a needle,' he thought to himself, 'I should also be prepared to meditate long and hard until I find my Maitreya.'

So he returned to his cave and meditated month after month for another three years; but again he was disappointed. In frustration, he left the cave a second time and started walking home. On the way, he saw a dog lying in his path. It was a miserable thing, and obviously in pain. Its body was covered with sores and maggots were eating at its flesh. Tomi's heart melted with deep compassion. He could not walk by and ignore the suffering of the dog, so he knelt down and ripped a piece off his shawl, intending to softly brush away the maggots. As he stretched out his hand to help the dog, the animal disappeared and Maitreya Buddha stood before him. Seeing Maitreya appear so suddenly, Tomi was amazed, surprised and puzzled.

'Maitreya! Where have you been for so long? I have been meditating and meditating and waiting and waiting for your appearance.'

'I have always been with you, but you have been too obsessed with your thoughts, your expectations and desires,' answered Maitreya gently. 'You were full of attachment to the idea of me. But I am not an idea, I am compassion itself. As long as you were attached with expectations, you could not see me; but while tending the wounded dog you lost all attachment and expectation and became full of unconditional compassion. Then you saw me no longer as a dog, but in my true form.'

'But,' protested Tomi, 'all that time I was meditating, chanting mantras, reciting holy scriptures, prostrating and visualizing you, all to no avail. All the rituals and all my effort for the best part of six years came to nothing.'

'Rituals are useless unless they are filled with boundless compassion of the heart,' Maitreya replied. 'If you don't believe me, carry me on your shoulders and walk through the market. You will find that no one can see me unless they have a heart full of compassion.'

So Tomi did exactly that. He carried Maitreya on his shoulders and walked through the busy market. No one noticed anything except one compassionate woman who stopped Tomi and said, 'You are carrying a wounded dog, it is in pain, let me help you. Let me do something to release this dog from its pain.'

Then and there, Tomi understood the truth and became enlightened. For the rest of his life, he swam in the sea of compassion for all sentient beings. He fulfilled his mother's hope and dream.

Acknowledgements

I express my gratitude to Satish Kumar and June Mitchell
who listened to my stories and put them into good English.
Without their help, this book would not have been possible.

Then I would like to thank Elaine Green of The Resurgence
Trust who kindly typed the stories and corrected proofs.

I would also thank *Resurgence & Ecologist* magazine where some
of these stories first appeared.

Then I would like to thank Sam Winston for his help with the
book and for his introduction.

Then I would like to thank all my students in Britain and around
the world who have encouraged and supported me in bringing
the message of compassion to a Western audience.

LAMA LHAKPA YESHE

Where it is unborn let it arise excellent, precious awakened mind.
Where it is born let it never decrease
May I ever encourage wisdom and compassion to rise higher
  and higher to Bodhicitta.

GESHE BEN